The Cat
Who
Taught Zen

The Cat
Who
Taught Zen

James Norbury

MICHAEL JOSEPH

Also by James Norbury

Big Panda and Tiny Dragon

The Journey: A Big Panda and Tiny Dragon Adventure

For the animals.

Teachers, messengers and most of all, friends.

Far from here, there was a city.

It sat upon the shores of a great river.

And was home to many thousands of people.

But this story is not about people.

This tale is about a Cat.

And on this cold autumn night, he is sheltering from the rain
with his very good friend, the Rat.

Rain spilled from the rooftops and bubbled down the gutters.
The people of the city hunched their shoulders against the
downpour and hurried to their homes.

The Cat watched them.

After a while, he turned to the Rat and said,
'I have been searching for many years.
But there is still so much I don't understand.'

'And what is it you're looking for?' asked the Rat.

The Cat sighed.

'I wish I knew.
Peace?
Acceptance?
Perhaps a way to make sense of the world . . .'

'Nothing too difficult then,' said the Rat, smiling kindly.

'But maybe I can help – I have heard that far from here,
deep within the maple forests that shroud the valley,
there is a single ancient pine tree.
And one who sits within its boughs will attain
a peace and understanding like no other.'

'Really?' asked the Cat.

The Rat nodded.

'Then my path is clear, I will leave at once.'

And bidding his friend farewell, he dropped soundlessly from the wall and followed the old road that led out of the city and towards the valley.

The Cat travelled for many hours.

As dusk fell across the land, he saw the glow of firelight coming from a distant cave.

He was sodden and cold and decided to take a chance.

The Cat peered cautiously into the cave.

To his suprise, a Hare was drying himself by the fire.

'Oh . . . hello,' said the Hare, a little startled.
'Come and join me. What brings you out here?'

As the last of the light faded,
the Cat gratefully seated himself by the fire.
'I am a spiritual traveller,' he said.
'I seek the ancient pine that grows amongst the maples.'

'Really?' said the Hare.
'And what brought you to follow this path?'

The Cat thought for a moment.
'I suppose it started many years ago, when I was just a kitten.'

'Once a year, a wise Dragon would visit the village where I lived.
The Dragon would talk with anyone who came to see him, and offer
guidance and wisdom.'

'I loved to visit him, every day.

But back then, I was mischievous and each time
I went to see the Dragon, I couldn't help but steal something
– a plum, some incense . . .

And on one occasion, I'm ashamed to say, his beautiful,
treasured bell.'

One day, when I went to see the Dragon, he was gone,
and in his place there was a small scroll with my name on it.'

Dear Kitten,

I very much enjoyed our conversations.

I know we will meet again.

Please don't forget to oil the bell now and then.
It will rust in this misty valley.

Ever your friend,
Dragon

'Well, as you can imagine I was overcome with guilt, but more importantly,
I couldn't believe how kindly the Dragon had treated me,
even though he knew all along I had been stealing from him.

This act of forgiveness had a profound effect on me.

It showed me how, without preaching, another's actions can inspire
change in those around them.

I became determined to continue the Dragon's good work.

That is how I came to follow this path.'

'I see,' said the Hare.

'So what did you do to start following the teachings of the Dragon?'

'Well, I started slowly,' said the Cat, 'and I made many mistakes,
but I think there are a few things which have made a real difference to me.'

'Please share,' said the Hare.

The Cat pondered a moment.

'Well,' he said, 'I still visit the Dragon every year, and each time he shares something with me that changes the way I think.

So I would have to say the first thing would be to . . .

. . . keep learning.

New ideas can help us grow and avoid
repeating the same mistakes.

It's easier to learn when you realize
life is always trying to teach you something.'

'Spend time in silence,

appreciate nature,

be mindful and seek peace.'

'Nature has no words

but it is trying to tell you something.'

'I once heard someone say,
it was not the journey or the destination that mattered most,
but the company.'

'Spend time with those who bring out the best in you.'

'What if you have no one?' asked the Hare.

'Wherever we go, we are our own companion,' said the Cat.

'And that is why we must try to be a good
friend to ourselves and treat ourselves with gentleness.

After all, we are the one we spend the most time with,
and we have a habit of taking our own opinions very seriously.'

'Kindness and gratitude are two qualities
I found difficult to learn, but they can help us in so many ways.

They cost nothing,
but their value cannot be overstated.'

'If you knew how much kindness could change your life,
you would practise it at every opportunity.

And, of course, if your kindness does not include
yourself or those you find difficult, it is incomplete.'

The two animals spoke long into the night until, at last,
they fell asleep around the dying embers of the fire.

Morning broke across the mountains, but when the Cat finally awoke, the Hare was gone.

In his place, there was some food carefully wrapped in a leaf.

The Cat smiled and gratefully ate the Hare's generous gift.

The morning sunlight had burned off the mists and
the Cat, stomach full, headed out along the mountain trail.

He had only been travelling for a few hours when a raucous cawing
broke the stillness.

Looking up, the Cat saw a Crow perched in a dead tree,
screeching and flapping its wings.

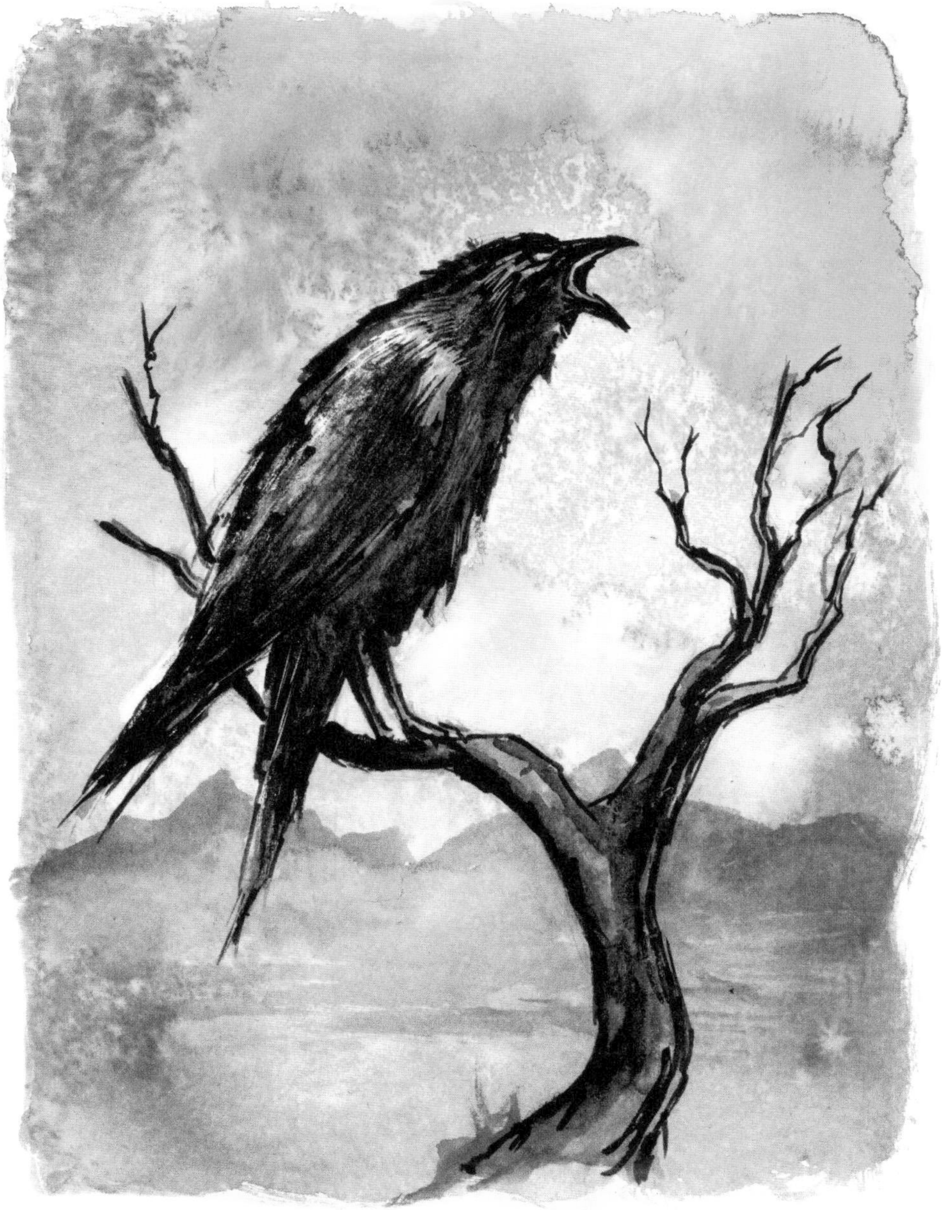

'Crow,' called the Cat.

'What is the matter?'

The Crow flew down to a low branch and eyed the Cat
with a tilted head.

'The nerve!' she squawked.

'Someone has stolen my shiny thing. I had a great deal of trouble
getting it and now someone has stolen it. I am furious.
I was going to use it to impress a friend!'

'Perhaps it's not the disaster you think it is,'
said the Cat.

'Pah!' scoffed the Crow. 'What would you know?'

'Well,' said the Cat, 'allow me to tell you a story about a little dragon I once knew, a descendant of the Great Dragon who used to visit my village.'

'His name was Tiny Dragon, and one day, while on a journey to meet
his friend Big Panda, he found the most exquisite thing;
a large, sea-green crystal that when gazed into, seemed to hold
all of the mysteries of the world.'

'But so absorbed did Tiny Dragon become, looking into the crystal
as he walked along, that he stumbled and dropped it on
his delicate dragon foot.'

'Well, needless to say he was in agony. He thought the bones
had been broken and was forced to halt his journey,
limping his way across the bridge to an abandoned hermitage.'

'Tiny Dragon, feeling sorry for himself, sat down on a rock.
It would probably take at least another day before he met
with Big Panda.'

'Hours passed and Tiny Dragon was wondering if it might be possible
to walk on his injured foot when the skies opened and rain fell
in torrents.'

'The storm raged.

Thunder and lightning wracked the skies and the earth shook.

Tiny Dragon huddled up in the corner of the hermitage and
hugged the crystal tightly to his chest.'

'When the storm had finally blown itself out, Tiny Dragon cautiously peered outside.

To his dismay he saw the bridge had collapsed.

He felt very unstable on his injured foot and decided he couldn't risk picking his way through the rubble.

Resigning himself to staying here overnight, he sat on a mossy stone and watched the bamboo swaying in the last whispers of the storm.'

'It was truly beautiful.'

'Night fell over the forest, and Tiny Dragon limped back
to the shelter of the hermitage.'

'As he sat staring out into the darkness, something was moving
amidst the trees.

Tiny Dragon felt a cold sense of dread.

But instead of hiding and despite his fear, Tiny Dragon watched
as a great beast, heavy and powerful, stepped into the moonlight.
He had never seen such a thing before, but knew from Big Panda's
stories it must be a Stag.

It paused for a moment, majestic and wild.

Tiny Dragon was overwhelmed to see such a magnificent sight.'

'Through Tiny Dragon's bravery,
darkness had been transformed into beauty,
and fear into wonder.'

Tiny Dragon watched until the Stag became one with
the leafy shadows. If he hadn't hurt his foot he would never
have seen one of the most incredible sights of his life.'

'Tiny Dragon climbed into his little makeshift bed
and thought to himself . . .

I wonder what wonders tomorrow will bring.'

'When morning came, Tiny Dragon decided his foot
was strong enough to continue.

But the crystal was becoming so heavy to carry that despite
how much he adored it, Tiny Dragon decided he would swap
it with a passing trader.'

'But the trader shook his head. "This is very common,"
he said, "and completely worthless."'

'But when Tiny Dragon thought about the experiences he'd had after finding the crystal

the beauty and the suffering,

the fear and the joy,

he was not so sure it was worthless to him.'

'So was the crystal beneficial?' mused the Cat.

'Who knows.

The way Tiny Dragon chose to look at it . . . perhaps.

My point, friend Crow, is that sometimes what we think is bad ends up good, and something we have always wanted, ends up harming us.'

'Flowers can bloom in the most unlikely of places.'

'I think I understand,' said the Crow.

'Fate leads us on a winding path and despite how bad a situation
may appear, we can never really know how it will turn out.

I'll try to remember that, then maybe I won't get so
upset when things don't go my way.'

The Crow nodded to the Cat, and with a beat of her great black wings,
took to the air.

The Cat watched until the Crow had disappeared into the mists.

At last he continued on his way, but before long,
gnarled oaks closed in and the Cat found himself in a dark,
tangled forest.

A rustling broke the quiet and from the brambles emerged
a solitary wolf cub, looking a little forlorn.

'Hello,' said the Cat, 'why are you out here alone?'

'The adults have gone hunting,' replied the Cub.
'They won't let me go – so I have to stay near the den.
I tried to sleep but I've had a very strange dream.'

'Would you like to tell me about it?' asked the Cat.

The Cub was reluctant at first, but with nothing better to do,
and feeling confused by the dream, he settled down next to the Cat.

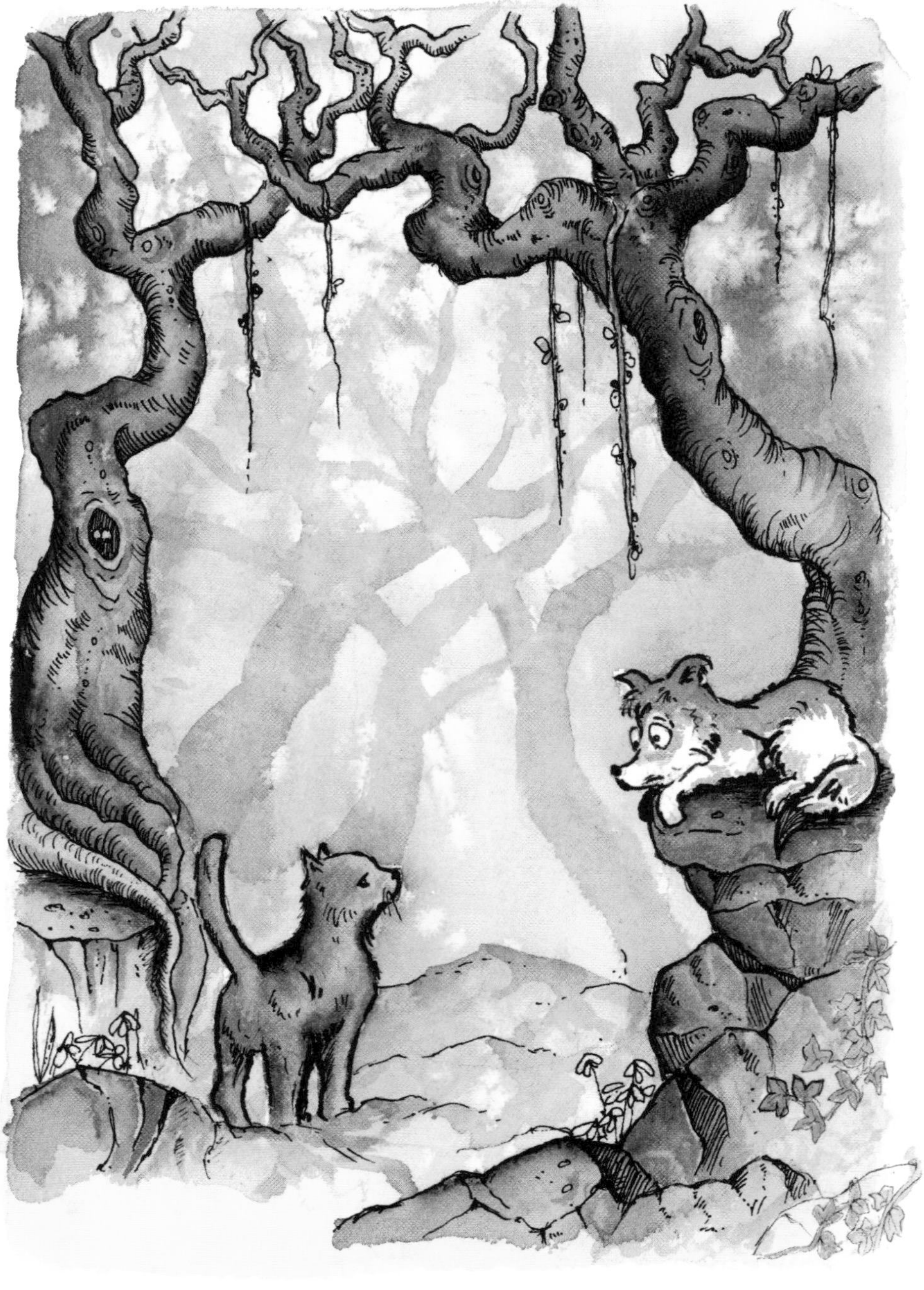

'In the dream, I'm being chased by a big dog.
I'm scared and I wish I was strong and powerful
like our pack leader. Then I wouldn't need to be scared of dogs.

And suddenly I'm magically transformed into a huge fearsome wolf.'

'So I chase the dog to scare it off, but quickly I feel hot and tired.

And then I see a river. It's flowing fast and cool across the land
and I really wish I could do the same.

Then suddenly . . .

I'm a river.'

'I flow fast and free, but very soon I merge with the ocean
and the excitement of being a river is gone.

Now I am still and deep, but I feel trapped and I'm getting bored.

I look up and see a great eagle soaring through the clouds. I think
how wonderful this would be and no sooner have I thought it than . . .

I'm an eagle!'

'Yet although I'm great and powerful, I am old and my life is nearing its end. Below me I see a wolf cub playing with her brother and sister, and I think about how much fun she's having, how she has her whole life ahead of her.

And then I wake up . . .'

The Cat listened in silence and when the Cub had finished he asked,
'So, what do you think it means?'

The Cub thought for a moment . . .

'Maybe,' he said quietly, 'we each have our own gifts to offer the world, and we should celebrate them, rather than wishing we had someone else's.'

The Cat nodded and smiled.

'Thank you,' said the Cub.

'I didn't do anything,' said the Cat.

'You listened,' said the Cub,
'and that made all the difference.'

The Cub ran back into the forest and the Cat continued along the path.

It was not long until the trees gave way to the grounds
of a great temple.

The Cat was walking along the shore
of a lake when he began to hear strange, garbled noises.

As he got closer, he saw a Monkey on a stone lantern
nervously chattering to himself.

When the Monkey spotted the Cat he peered at him intently and started to bombard him with questions and nonsense.

'Who are you?

I'm hungrier than I was.

Do you want something from me?

It's going to rain soon . . .

Why are you here?'

'I am here,' said the Cat, 'because I seek the ancient pine.
It is said that those who sit within its boughs
will attain the greatest peace.'

'Peace!' said the Monkey. 'If only I could have a little peace.
My thoughts – they're driving me crazy.'

'Come and sit with me,' said the Cat.

'This lake,' he continued, 'is fed by a river.
If you listen very carefully you can hear it.'

The Monkey tipped his head to one side and listened.

But he could hear nothing.
He focused harder, straining his ears for
even the faintest sound of running water.

'It's no good,' he said eventually, 'I simply cannot hear it.
Maybe I need big long cat ears like you?'

'Whether you could hear the river or not doesn't matter,' said the Cat. 'But tell me, for those last few moments, how busy was your mind?'

And the Monkey realized, for the first time in as long as he could remember, that his racing thoughts had calmed.

'For a moment there,' said the Cat,
'you were so focused on listening that the past, the future,
and all your thoughts about them ceased to exist.

It was just a glimpse, but you have seen the peace that is within us all.'

The Monkey didn't move, he didn't speak.

He just watched the swallows skimming the water and
felt the autumn breeze against his fur.

The Cat left him to enjoy his peace and
walked on through the temple gardens.

Nestled in the grass he saw an ancient Tortoise, hidden in her shell.

The Tortoise's head slowly emerged.

'Hello,' said the Cat. 'This place is beautiful.'

'It was,' said the Tortoise.

'But I tire of its cherry groves and am weary of the motionless lakes,
the incessant babbling of streams and the relentless drone of the wind
in the trees.

The buildings never change and each day brings the same
sun and rain and clouds . . .

and so it goes on . . .

and on and on.'

'You are tired of life,' said the Cat.

The Tortoise nodded.
'With any luck, my time will come and I can leave this tiresome world.'

'I have something which might help you,'
said the Cat, dipping his paw in the damp ash of a temple lantern.

He then wrote upon a large flat stone.

Each moment is a unique place
in the world just for you.

Savour it now,
for you can never visit it again.

The Tortoise peered at the Cat's words,
and taking her time – as Tortoises do – turned to the Cat,
a tear on her cheek.

'I had never thought of it like that,' she said.

'All I wanted was for this moment to be over,
hoping the next would be better and somehow fulfil me
. . . but it never happened.

And now I read this – I see why.'

'I have seen a lot, friend Cat.
A hundred summers, a thousand temples, a million stars,
but have I ever really, truly smelt a flower?
Well . . . I cannot wait to do so.

Thank you.'

And as the Cat walked away, the Tortoise was left
not just with her flower, but with a sense of hope.

The Cat felt something powerful stir deep within him,
for he felt he had done more good since leaving the city
than he had in years of being shut away, focusing on himself.

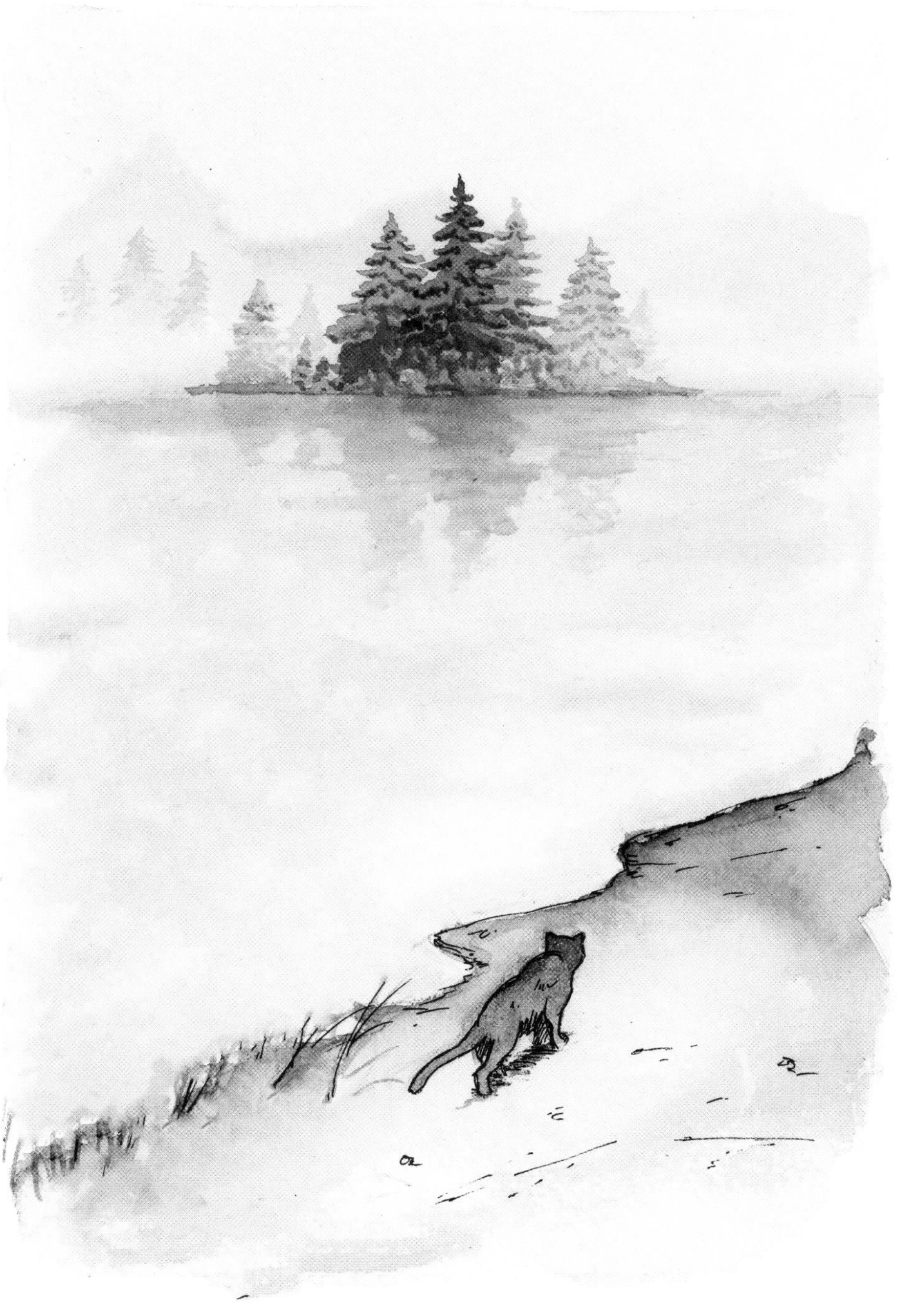

The light was fading.

The Cat was just beginning to think about stopping for the night
when an explosion of teeth and claws burst from the trees.

The Tiger raised its massive claw and snarled.

'Ah,' said the Cat, 'here opens the gateway to suffering.'

'What!?' roared the Tiger. 'You should be terrified.
I could kill you here and now.'

The Cat eyed the furious creature for a moment.
'You are creating your own pain, friend Tiger.

You think that by besting me you will feel mighty and strong,
but it will not bring you the satisfaction you are seeking.

It will never be enough, and you will live angry and unfulfilled.

If I am mistaken, do tell me, but I imagine the last time
you did this your victory was hollow and short-lived?'

The Tiger paused.

He thought back to the countless times he had done this same thing,
relishing his power and ferocity and the terror in his victims.

But just like the Cat said, it had never lasted,
and he had quickly set out to find more ways to strike fear
into the creatures of the forest.

The Cat watched the Tiger's fury dissolve.
His claws and fangs retreated and his eyes softened.

An expression of confusion and even curiosity spread across his face.
For what the Tiger had been so sure of just a few seconds ago,
he was no longer certain about.

'Ah,' said the Cat, 'here opens the gateway to peace.'

The Tiger made no sound. He looked at one of his great paws, sheathing and unsheathing its dagger-like claws.

'Maybe I was wrong,' he said. 'I have been angry for so long. I thought that being better than those around me would somehow make me feel good.'

'Just the idea of not trying to be the best feels so good –
so calming – I somehow feel I have come back to myself.'

Fascinated by what the Cat had said and
the peace that had settled over him,
the Tiger asked if he might accompany the Cat for a while.

The Cat agreed, and after spending
the night in the boughs of a great oak,
they were ready to continue towards the valley.

The next morning, mist had fallen across the land and the Cat was concerned he would become lost. But the Tiger knew the area well. 'Sit on my back,' he said, 'we will make good time.'

'Have you always travelled alone?' asked the Tiger.

'In my heart, yes,' answered the Cat.
'But I am learning to change.'

'I have never had a friend,' said the Tiger.
'How odd that we two strangers should get along.'

'Our souls are not so different,' said the Cat.
'Deep down, we need the same things.'

'It's strange,' said the Cat, 'I was talking with a crow yesterday about how you never know how things are going to turn out.

There is every chance I could have been your dinner last night, and now, here you are, helping me on my journey.'

'True,' said the Tiger, 'but your actions are motivated by kindness, and I think perhaps the universe is looking out for you.'

This made the Cat pause, and again, he thought back to his time in the city and how much he had been focused on himself and his path.

'Maybe,' he said after a time.

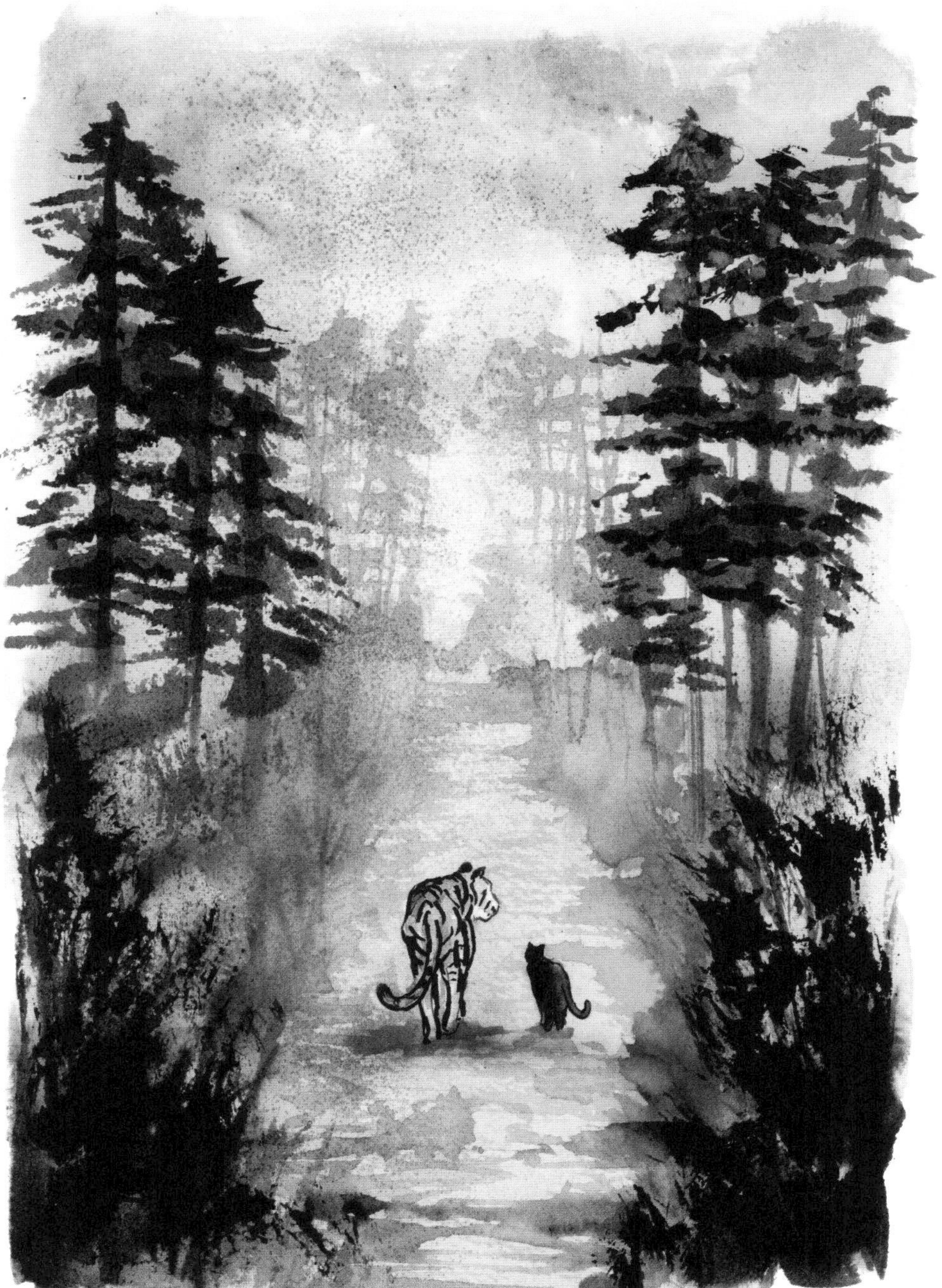

'But one thing I am certain of,' said the Cat, 'is that the more I have
gone out of my way to help others, the richer my life has become.'

'Like sowing seeds,' said the Tiger.
'A little work, perhaps, but so much to reap.'

They journeyed on for much of the morning until they came to
a fork in the road.

One path rose sharply upwards, the terrain rocky and treacherous.

The other, broad and devoid of obstacles, continued through the mist.

A signpost stood in the fork.

'That way to the Great Tree,' said the Tiger, gesturing
to the more difficult route.

'The obstacle is often the path,' thought the Cat.

The Cat and the Tiger sat down in the long grass. The Tiger turned
to the Cat and said 'I can't stop thinking about your words.
I can feel something has started to change inside me and
I want to walk a new path.

But I am not "quite" ready to begin.

I have seen the monks at the temple, and they have special cushions
and incense and candles. They also have books brimming with wisdom.
I shall need to acquire these things before I start.'

'That signpost,' said the Cat 'is not the destination.
It simply points to it . . .

Likewise, the books are not the way, although
they can help you find it. Just like the signpost,
if you spend all your time studying it you will
never get where you're going.'

'Let me tell you a story.

There was a lady with no money, who each day would sit on the side of the road and hope that strangers would give her coins so that she might eat. She lived that way for many years. I would often visit her.'

'Although we didn't speak

we understood each other.'

'One day I noticed that the box she always sat on was cracked, and inside I could see the glimmer of coins.

Well, I knew these would really help her so I nudged the box with my nose, but she just smiled and stroked me.'

'Each day I nudged at the box and mewed until one day
she became curious and looked more carefully.

When she spotted what was in it she was overwhelmed.'

'The first thing she did was rush out to get me food and a blanket.
She was so very kind.

She doted on me, as though I was the source of her good fortune.

But I was only the messenger.'

'The lady had possessed the treasure all along.
She just needed someone to show her where to look.

And even though she was no longer poor, she did not change.
She was simply able to do more of the things that were important
to her.

She helped those who needed it, for she was wise and she knew that
was where happiness dwelt.'

The Tiger sat in thought for a while then turned to the Cat.

'So you are saying that I should start walking the path right now,
even though I don't feel ready?'

'It is better to begin the journey, make some mistakes and
correct your course, than to wait until everything is perfect
and never even start.'

'I understand,' said the Tiger.
'And so I think it is time to walk my new path alone.
Thank you, Cat.'

'So which path will you take?' asked the Cat, looking at the two routes.

'Neither,' said the Tiger, turning towards the forest.
'I will walk my own path.'

The Cat watched the Tiger disappear into the leafy
shadows and smiled to himself.

The way ahead looked treacherous and difficult and
despite his eagerness to get to the ancient tree,
he decided to rest and continue in the morning.

It was raining when the Cat awoke, but he pressed on regardless.
The icy downpour soaked his fur, chilling him to the bones.

But few things can deter a cat once it has made up its mind.

By midday, the Cat had reached the higher slopes
of the valley and he was sure he could see the tree the
Rat had spoken of.

Its thick, gnarled limbs towered above the rest of the forest.

The Cat felt a surge of excitement.

He made his way down the mountain and into the maple forest.

The Cat paused for a moment to listen to the sound of the rain
pattering on the canopy.

This was indeed a magical place – he could feel it.

Up ahead the Cat noticed something moving in the path.

As he got closer he saw it was a Kitten
utterly absorbed in chasing autumn leaves.

The Cat moved closer until the Kitten, despite being intensely focused on a particularly badly behaved twig, noticed the Cat, and dived under a pile of leaves.

'Hello,' grinned the Kitten. 'What are you doing out here?'

'I am on an important task,' said the Cat, without slowing his pace.

'You have the eyes of someone who is searching for something,'
said the Kitten, bounding after him.
'Are you hungry? What are you looking for?'

'I don't think you would understand,' said the Cat,
eager to be on his way.

'Try me,' said the Kitten, optimistically. 'I'm smarter than I look.'

'I am very sorry,' said the Cat, 'maybe another time.'

'But where are your friends?' asked the Kitten.

'This is not a journey where I need friends,'
replied the Cat, a little impatience breaking into his voice.

'I am quite happy on my own.'

'But friends are like magic,' said the Kitten.
'When you share something good with a friend,
you somehow get more than if you'd kept it to yourself.'

'And if something isn't right, just telling your friend can make it seem
better, even though they might not know how to fix it.'

The Cat looked down at the Kitten,
who was clearly enjoying himself, and sighed.

'If only it were that simple. But if you will please excuse me,
I must be on my way, and for this particular "magic",
solitude is necessary.'

The Cat increased his pace, leaving the Kitten to his leaves,
and continued along the trail.

He slightly regretted his brusque treatment of the Kitten, but this
was important. There would be time for that kind of thing later.

And then . . .

finally

rising from the forest floor was the most magnificent tree
the Cat had ever seen.

It was everything the Rat had spoken of.
A magnificent specimen and older than the forest itself.

The Cat could sense a powerful spiritual energy.

He approached the tree and with the utmost care, climbed up into the low-hanging branches.

He carefully selected a dry spot and sat down to meditate.

'Ah . . .' thought the Cat to himself, 'this is it.
This is what I have been searching for.'

He closed his eyes and allowed the power of the tree to work upon him.

At first the Cat was sure he could feel something, an energy,
a spiritual power, but as he sat there, he began to think the feeling
was no different to when he sat under the old ash tree
that grew outside the city.

'Perhaps it just takes a while,' thought the Cat to himself.
'Maybe my mind is not empty enough.'

But time passed, and still the Cat felt nothing.

Until, suddenly . . .

With a crash of pine needles and dead wood,
something sodden and furry fell from above,
slamming into him and knocking him off the branch.

The Cat leapt backwards, hissing and spitting.

'How dare you disturb my time of peace and calm!'

But the Kitten simply rolled onto its front and clumsily stood.

It showed no fear and no complaint.

As the Cat watched the Kitten, something began to change within him.

And it had nothing to do with a magical tree.

And he smiled a broad, sincere smile.

A smile he had not known for many years.

And as the Cat sat in the rain, watching the wet Kitten
playfully chasing leaves across the forest floor,
he finally understood why he was here and what he was missing.

He realized that through all the years of
solitary practice he had been focused only on himself.

And he thought back over his journey and all the creatures
he had helped to bring a little peace to:

the Hare, the Crow, the Tortoise, the Cub, the Monkey and the Tiger

and he realized that this was never about a tree.

This was about taking all the things he had learned over his life,
all the gifts he had been given, and sharing them.

And that the small things he'd ignored were in fact
the things he should have been paying the most attention to.

A sense of deep caring for the little Kitten spread through him and he felt truly at peace for the first time in many years.

No yearning.
No desire to search outside himself.

Who would have guessed it would have taken a clumsy,
bedraggled kitten and its gentle, unconditional kindness
to show him the way.

It was not lost on the Cat that just yesterday he was talking about
how you never knew what would end up being good and bad for you.

'Thank you,' said the Cat. 'You teach what words could never explain.'

The Kitten tried to grab its own tail and, slightly disappointed,
turned to the Cat. 'I don't understand,' he said.

'Your willingness to not understand – that's your strength,'
said the Cat.

'Here I am trying to understand everything, trying to seek the truth.

And you're the one who is joyfully in this moment, not questioning
why – seeing the value in the simple things around you and trying to
build friendships.'

The rain gave way to mist and the sun hung low in the sky.

'I'd love to be your friend,' said the Kitten.

'And I yours,' said the Cat.

They sat under the shelter of the great tree for a while.
Then the Kitten turned to the Cat.

'So, did you find what you were looking for?' he asked.
'I think so,' replied the Cat.

'I've learned that what we want is seldom what we need.
And what we need is almost never what we want.'

The Kitten looked at the Cat, confused.

'Well,' said the Cat, 'the things we don't want can challenge us and frustrate us. Often we wish there was a "magical" solution that would fix all our problems.

But sometimes, it's these problems and the struggles that force us to face ourselves, and in the process of doing this, we learn about ourselves, we become stronger and we start to see what is truly valuable.

Then we can look at the world with new eyes.'

'Of course,' said the Cat, 'life doesn't always go to plan,
and we don't always have the presence and wisdom to
learn from our problems.'

'But the fact that you don't always know how things may ultimately
turn out can bring light to dark places.

The idea that the problem you are currently facing could end up
having something positive hidden within it can help you through
the experience.'

The Cat got up, took one last look at the ancient pine,
and prepared to leave.

The Kitten's face fell as he thought of his new friend leaving him,
but perhaps the Cat was right. Maybe there might
be a hidden benefit to being alone again.

'Are you going home now?' asked the Kitten quietly.

'I came here because there were things I did not understand,'
said the Cat, 'and despite what has happened here,
I'm afraid I still have much to discover.'

'But one thing I do know, friend Kitten,
is that whatever lies ahead,
it will be better with you alongside.'

'The secret to a beautiful life is not just
in an ancient tree or a star-filled sky.

It is in the leaves and the mud and the rain.

In you and me and in the bustling city I left far behind.'

The End

Afterword

Zen can be a confusing idea. It can conjure up a range of images from white, minimal apartments to solitary monks sitting in silence. To me, it is simply the cultivation of a way of being which brings more peace and wisdom into our lives.

One of the most fundamental aspects of zen is that it is almost impossible to explain, much like the taste of a peach, and the simplest way to understand it is to experience it. Unfortunately, its deeper meanings can be elusive to most of us.

In this book I have tried to approach zen in a more practical way that takes some of its ideas and stories and makes them more accessible and useful on a day-to-day level. To do this I have selected a number of traditional zen stories which have been used for hundreds of years to point towards ideas without literally explaining them.

I spent a great deal of time studying zen stories before settling on a selection I thought would work well in the book. Some of the tales are new and although I hope they capture the spirit of zen, are of my own devising.

I chose the stories I did mostly because they have ideas which you can immediately integrate into your own day, irrespective of what you are doing. For example, in the Monkey's story, he realizes that just by shifting his focus for a moment, the whole world can change – this is something we can experiment with at any time. Likewise, I'm sure many readers have felt like the Tortoise, but I find the idea that this moment that I'm in right now will never be repeated helps to add something deeply profound to our everyday, mundane experiences. You could consider it right now while you read this.

Many of us feel hesitant to start something new and tend to wait until the time is right, just like the Tiger. I feel this way when I start to create a new picture or book or write an afterword, but I have learned to give myself permission to start messily with no expectation and somehow, each time, things just seem to work themselves out.

I have also allowed zen philosophy to influence the art of the book. Although many of the images are in a traditional style, some use a technique called sumi-e which was used centuries ago in East Asia and involves painting with black ink on special papers. This type of work is extremely spontaneous and instinctive and does not really allow the artist to be fussy and overly detailed. The rich black brushstrokes on the delicate rice paper are supremely enjoyable and the way these materials work together creates all kinds of random yet wonderful patterns and effects.

Nature really is contributing to the final image, and it really teaches you to relinquish control (another wonderful zen concept). The pictures on pages 15, 17, 19, 21, 46, 53, 59, 89, 106, 109, 110, 124 and 169 use this technique.

Aside from retelling these stories, I also wanted to have an overarching tale which not only unified the stories into a single narrative, but also showed an individual's journey and the struggles they experience trying to follow a spiritual path.

During the Cat's travels he meets many animals and although he aids each one by sharing a version of an ancient zen story, he is also helping himself, for all life is connected, and when we benefit others, we cannot help but benefit ourselves.

The Cat finds it very easy to offer these creatures advice, but not so easy to apply it to himself and even starts to become annoyed towards the end of the story when he sees the Kitten as an obstacle to his enlightenment. But as the old expression goes:

The obstacle IS the path.

The Kitten was the last thing the Cat wanted, but the one thing he really needed.

During my own work day, one of my cats likes to pace back and forth across my work area, blocking off my monitor, walking on my paintings and generally doing anything she can to get attention. I am very tempted to shut her out of the room – I've got important work to do! But this is exactly the messenger I need – she reminds me to stop and stroke her and appreciate her tiny feline form. And one day she'll be gone, and I don't want to recall all the times I shut her out the room because I was too busy.

So where is the zen?

Much like the Tiger, it's easy to become seduced by the idea that the path to peace requires retreats, meditation, gurus and incense. Of course, these things can certainly help, but one of the things I like most about zen philosophy is how empowering it is to the individual. You can start on your own, right this second.

There is something beautiful in the drone of traffic or the stained concrete of an old tower block. As Big Panda says, 'There is beauty everywhere, but sometimes it's difficult to see.'

If you can take just thirty seconds to really feel the fabric of your clothes or listen to the noises outside your window, you can, like the Monkey, be transported to another state of mind. If, just for a second, your mind stops and the experience takes over, then you have encountered zen.

If you can practise this whenever you remember it, it may start to bring a little more peace into your life. Even zen monks do not spend all day in meditation, the majority of their time is spent doing tasks, but they attempt to do them with a deliberate, aware-mind state.

If you could take one thing away from this book, I would ask you to try and remember that good things often come out of seemingly bad things.

Lotus flowers are significant in Buddhism – in part because they grow out of filth.

If you can embed this idea in your mind, I think life can become more joyful as it can take the sting out of the negative experiences that visit us daily. This is not always easy, and some experiences are so overwhelmingly painful that trying to see the good in them is simply not always possible, but if you start small and try to develop it as a habit it can start to change the way you see the world, and ultimately increase your own happiness.

And if you feel uncertain about any of the ideas in this book, that's good – just like for the Tiger in the story, confusion is the first sign you are about to change.

MICHAEL JOSEPH

UK | USA | Canada | Ireland | Australia
India | New Zealand | South Africa

Michael Joseph is part of the Penguin
Random House group of companies
whose addresses can be found at
global.penguinrandomhouse.com.

Penguin
Random House
UK

First published in Great Britain by
Michael Joseph, 2023
001

Set in Bauer Bellefair

Colour origination by Altaimage, London
Printed and bound in Italy by L.E.G.O. S.p.A.

A CIP catalogue record for this book is
available from the British Library

ISBN: 978-0-241-64015-9

www.greenpenguin.co.uk

MIX
Paper | Supporting
responsible forestry
FSC® C018179

Penguin Random House is committed to a
sustainable future for our business, our readers
and our planet. This book is made from Forest
Stewardship Council® certified paper.